Purple Ronnie's

Little Book of

Football

by Purple Ronnie

First published 2002 by Boxtree
an imprint of Pan Macmillan Ltd
Pan Macmillan, 20 New Wharf Road, London N1 9RR
Basingstoke and Oxford
Associated companies throughout the world
www.panmacmillan.com

ISBN 0 7522 6529 6

9 8 7 6

A CIP catalogue record for this book is available from
the British Library.

Text by Giles Andreae
Illustrations by Janet Cronin
Printed and bound in Hong Kong

a poem for a
↓
Football Fan

Some blokes would think that
   their dreams had come true
If a naked girl walked
           through the door
But footie fans know
That the best thing in life
Is just watching your
   football team score

Be Prepared

Remember - you will not want to take your eyes off the telly for at least 2 hours, so make sure you are fully prepared beforehand

potty for emergency wee
BEER
Pork Scratch-ings
BEER
loads of beer

a poem about ↓

Football

Football is full of surprises
And all sorts of curious laws
Like holding your bits
When they're taking free
kicks
And snogging each player
who scores

Interesting Fact

If football didn't exist, most men wouldn't have anything to say to each other

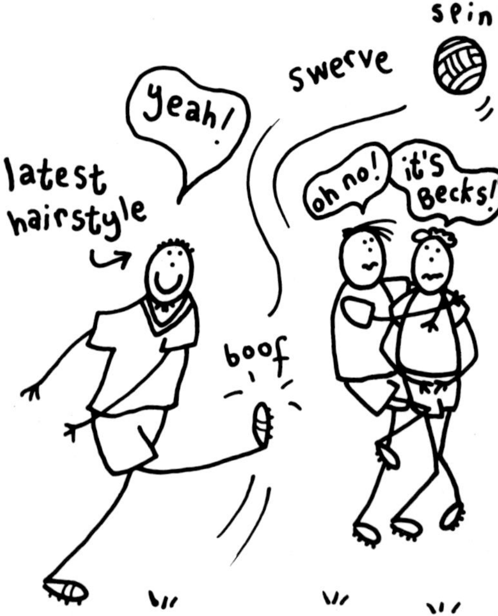
spin
swerve
yeah!
latest hairstyle
oh no!
it's Becks!
boof

a poem about

David Beckham

Line up any team you like
– His right foot will
              wreck 'em
He's a genius of football
And his name is
         David Beckham
              ☆

Men's Brains

Here is a map of
a typical man's
brain

Girls and Football

Some girls love
watching football too

a poem about
↓
The World Cup

It's fun to go out
drinking
And I like to fill my
belly
But there's nothing more
fantastic
Than the World Cup
on the telly!

Special Tip

It's a good idea to reinforce your TV before an important match

Sneaky Tip

If your girlfriend gets cross because you watch too much football- tell her that jumping up and down all day is good exercise

a poem about ↓

Football Fans

Why do men talk about
football
When most of them don't
even play?
They chant and they cheer
And swig loads of beer
And just watch it on
telly all day

Weird Fact

When men get together to go to a football match they immediately turn into 5 year old schoolboys

Dreams

Football fans only
ever have 2 dreams

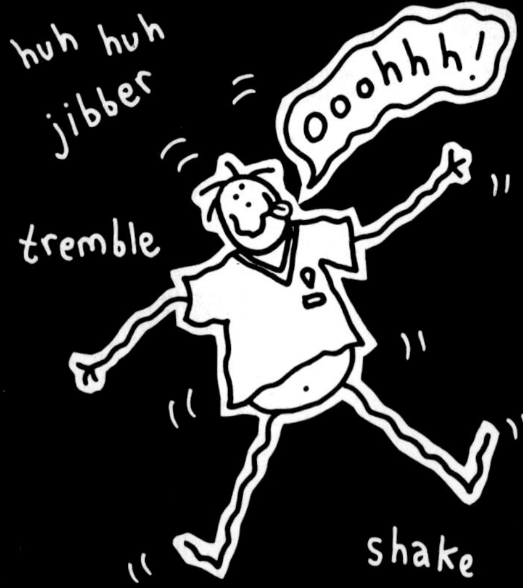
huh huh
jibber
Ooohhh!
tremble
shake

a poem about a
↓
Football Nutter

Before the start of
every match

You start to shake and
stutter

Cos you're a footie
maniac

-An utter Footall
Nutter!

<u>Singing</u>

Watching football is the only time most men don't feel silly singing

Sad Fact

Some men spend their life savings following their team all around the world

a poem about

Football Addicts

Some people have to eat
chocolate
And some people crave
cups of tea
But others just have to
crack open the lagers
And worship their team
on T.V.

Deep_Question

Why do men shout at the players on the telly when they know they can't hear them?

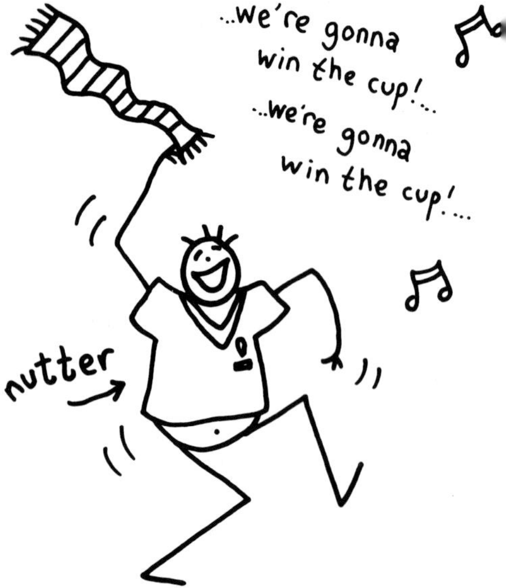
...we're gonna win the cup!...
...we're gonna win the cup!...
nutter

a poem about being
↓
Football Mad

Some people think it's
magic

And some just think it's
sad

But you don't give a
monkey's bum

Cos you're so Football
Mad!

Crafty Tip

Always order your takeaway before the match to avoid the half-time rush

blah
blah
HALFTIME
15 vindaloos
20 onion bhajees
50 popadoms
and a
korma
for the
lady
ring
ring
STAR OF INDIA
sprint

Crying

Football is one of the only things that men don't mind crying about

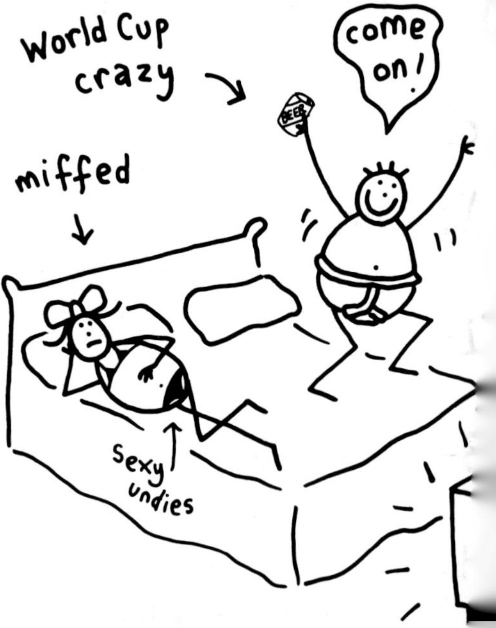

World Cup
crazy
come on!
BEER
miffed
sexy
undies

a poem about a
↓
World Cup Fan

It's usually not very
tricky
Enticing your man
into bed
But when the World Cup
is on telly
He'd much rather watch
that instead